Dedication

For my dearest mother, who taught me that I can achieve anything when I decide it's important. And for telling me not to be a baby.

Contents

DINKcuisine

INTRODUCTION

When people ask about my ethnicity, I generally respond that I am Italian. The truth is that I am half French, half Italian. However, as with many families, one culture often dominates most of the social aspects of day-to-day life, especially food! And for me, that's Italian.

My mother, Celeste Camagna, to whom this book is dedicated, is the best cook I've ever known. She taught me the most important cooking lesson of my life at a very early age: Exceptional food contains at least one of these things—enough salt, plenty of mayonnaise, a splash of half-and-half, and copious amounts of butter. I add eggs, cream cheese, and sour cream to that list as well when people ask me my secret to tasty food. But that's just because I want to be like Mom.

If you do a decent amount of cooking, chances are you're used to cooking recipes with four to six servings, just because that's how the vast majority of recipes in the United States are written. When I learned that the average American household contains just over two people (US Census, 2020), I realized that I wasn't the only one who was overcooking. Unless you really love leftovers or are exceptionally efficient at meal planning, you're probably sick of doing fractions to carve recipes down to create a meal for two people. This cookbook will remove the guesswork for you.

My other hope for this cookbook is that it exposes you to a side of Italian food you don't normally experience. There are five chapters aligned to honor the basic courses you'd find at a traditional Italian table: Antipasti, Primi, Secondi, Insalata, and Dolce, and a sixth chapter, Supplementare, with additional guidance. Each chapter offers four recipes, all of which can be prepared with widely available ingredients and minimal effort.

The order in which you prepare and serve the recipes isn't important, and I'm not suggesting you always prepare five courses per meal. While my appetite has been legendary at times, I typically make one or two recipes per day to maintain a healthy lifestyle. My hope is that these recipes will become part of your repertoire any time you crave something savory. Or sweet. Mix and match them to create memorable meals for anyone you care about—and especially, yourself.

XO,

Antipasti

Preceded by the aperitivo, such as nuts and olives—and Manhattans, if you're a Camagna, antipasti is the course that welcomes you to the table and rewards your patience for hours of anticipatory hunger. Antipasti is the course I most fondly remember from childhood, especially during the holidays.

My cousins, Emily and Margaret, and I would drop any rambunctious activity in progress and immediately race to the table to take our seats when called for dinner. Our grandmother, Madeline, expertly prepared numerous dishes for our gluttonous enjoyment. I can't think of a holiday where we didn't outeat the rest of the family.

Caulifiori Tots

Fiori is Italian for "flowers." Cheesy? Quite! This keto winner substitutes carb-heavy potatoes with riced cauliflower to create light and salty tots that are scrumptious alone, and divine when dunked in tomato sauce (page 63). Forgot to buy riced cauliflower? Try rice! Or steam some broccoli and shred it in the food processor.

SERVES: 2 I PREP TIME: 5 MIN I COOK TIME: 30 MIN I TOTAL TIME: 35 MIN

12 ounces riced cauliflower, steamed

1 large egg, beaten

1 cup shredded mozzarella

1 cup freshly grated parmesan

⅔ cup pork rind crumbs

2 tablespoons Italian parsley, chopped

¼ teaspoon salt

1 teaspoon Italian seasoning

½ teaspoon black pepper

½ cup tomato sauce

1. Preheat oven to 400F. Line a baking sheet with parchment paper.

2. Place riced cauliflower on a clean kitchen towel and squeeze to release as much water as possible. Transfer cauliflower to a large bowl and add remaining ingredients. Mix well.

3. Roll about 1 tablespoon of mixture into a tater-tot shape with your hands and place on baking sheet. Repeat to form remaining tots. Bake for 30 minutes, until tots are golden. Sprinkle with a little more salt and serve warm with tomato sauce.

Pesto Deviled Eggs

Wondering what to do with the resto your pesto? Buy some already shelled, hard boiled eggs and get devilish!

SERVES: 2 | PREP TIME: 5 MIN | TOTAL TIME: 5 MIN

6 shelled, hard boiled eggs

1 teaspoon garlic salt

2 tablespoons sour cream

2 tablespoons mayonnaise

3 tablespoons prepared pesto (page 61)

1. Cut each egg in half and scoop the yolks into a bowl. Arrange the egg whites on a platter.

2. To the yolks, add garlic salt, sour cream, mayonnaise, and 3 tablespoons pesto and combine with a fork.

3. Use a spatula to load the egg mixture into a piping bag and pipe about a tablespoon into each egg white.

4. Arrange eggs on a platter, garnished with basil leaves, shredded parmesan, and pine nuts.

Grape and Mortadella Crostini

Delicate shallots, creamy mascarpone, and sweet grapes balance mouthwatering mortadella, the king of Italian cold cuts. No baguette? Find store-bought crostini at an Italian market, or mound this savory mixture on your favorite crackers.

SERVES: 2 | PREP TIME: 10 MIN | COOK TIME: 8 MIN | TOTAL TIME: 18 MIN

1 baguette, cut into 12 ¼-inch slices

2 tablespoons extra-virgin olive oil

¼ teaspoon salt

⅓ pound mortadella, diced

18 seedless red grapes

2 tablespoons shallot

¼ cup mascarpone cheese, room temperature

2 tablespoons pistachios, finely chopped

1. Preheat the oven to 400F. Lay the baguette slices on a baking sheet. Brush each slice of baguette with olive oil and sprinkle each with a pinch of salt. Bake until golden brown and crispy, about 8 minutes. Remove the crostini from the tray and set aside to cool.

2. In a small food processor, add mortadella, 12 grapes, and shallot and pulse until combined.

3. Spread an equal layer of mascarpone on each crostino, then top them with a generous spoonful of the mixture. Halve the remaining 6 grapes. Top each crostino with a halved grape and a pinch of chopped pistachio.

Sausage and Pepper Bites

One of the world's greatest flavor combos makes the perfect, bite-sized app. Doesn't everything taste better on a toothpick?

SERVES: 2 | PREP TIME: 10 MIN | COOK TIME: 30 MIN | TOTAL TIME: 40 MIN

5 links Italian sausage

1 onion, peeled and quartered

1 package mini sweet peppers

1 tablespoon olive oil

1 teaspoon salt

1 teaspoon pepper

1. Preheat oven to 400F. Cut Italian sausage links into 1 inch pieces and place them on a parchment lined baking sheet.

2. Place onions and peppers on a separate parchment lined baking sheet, coat with olive oil, season with salt and pepper, and roast with sausage for 25–30 minutes.

3. Blot any accumulated grease from sausage.

4. Quarter the mini peppers. Separate the layers of onion.

5. Place a piece of sausage, a slice of onion, and a slice of pepper on a toothpick. Repeat until all sausage is used. Place the completed bites on a bed of arugula and garnish with shaved cheese and extra peppers and onions.

Primi

When my husband, Mark, emphatically expresses approval, he'll often exclaim, "Primo!" The first warm course of a traditional Italian meal, primi dishes deserve such praise, as they ooze comfort and contentment.

My family is from Piedmont, one of the Northernmost regions of Italy. The cuisine of Piedmont resembles the snow-capped mountains of the Alps, an extreme departure from the tomato-laden delights of the Southern regions. These recipes provide the freshness and familiarity of those red sauces with the creaminess and richness of the white sauces we enjoy in the North.

While primi range from soup to risotto, my favorite is pasta. A box of pasta is shelf stable, naturally vegetarian, and the chameleon of carbohydrates. Envelop half a box of pasta in dairy and a little ground meat, and dinner for two is finito.

Creamy Truffle Rigatoni

Truffle-infused cream sauce clings to every luscious bite. Rigatoni, penne, mostaccioli.... If it ends in a vowel, it will be delicious.

SERVES: 2 | PREP TIME: 5 MIN | COOK TIME: 20 MIN | TOTAL TIME: 25 MIN

8 ounces mezzi rigatoni (or penne)

1 ½ cups heavy cream

8 ounces truffle brie, rind removed

½ cup parmesan cheese, grated

1. Boil pasta in salted water for 12 minutes.

2. Warm heavy cream over medium low. Dice truffle brie into small pieces and add to warm cream. Stir until brie is completely melted. Remove from heat and add parmesan. Stir until combined.

3. Drain pasta. Fold in truffle cream sauce until all the pasta is coated and creamy.

Pasta Con Spinaci

Ricotta and spinach are phenomenal together. Combine them with Italian sausage and ground beef and your pasta shells are officially #yum! For an unexpected twist, replace the spinach with braised kale or chard.

SERVES: 2 | PREP TIME: 10 MIN | COOK TIME: 20 MIN | TOTAL TIME: 30 MIN

8 ounces medium pasta shells

½ pound bulk Italian sausage

½ pound ground beef

8 ounces frozen spinach, thawed

1 cup ricotta

1 tablespoon garlic paste (or minced garlic)

1 teaspoon salt

4 tablespoons half-and-half

1 cup tomato sauce (page 63)

2 tablespoons Parmesan cheese, grated

1. Preheat oven to 350F. Cook pasta two minutes less than the recommended cooking time, and drain.

2. Brown sausage and ground beef; drain the meat on paper towels to remove excess grease.

3. As the meat cools, squeeze as much water from the thawed spinach as possible. In a small bowl, combine spinach, garlic, ricotta, salt, and half-and-half.

4. Add the cooled meat, tomato sauce, and pasta. Combine and transfer to an 8x8 baking dish. Dust the top with Parmesan cheese.

5. Bake for 20 minutes and allow to set for 5 minutes before serving.

Lasagna Bianche di Pollo

Ground chicken spiced with fennel offers the delicious notes of Italian sausage without the extra fat. If you lack the time for a layered lasagne dish, cook the ground chicken and combine all the ingredients with your pasta of choice.

SERVES: 2 | PREP TIME: 25 MIN | COOK TIME: 30 MIN | TOTAL TIME: 55 MIN

½ pound ground chicken breast

½ teaspoon salt

1 teaspoon ground black pepper

1 ½ cups grated parmesan cheese

1 teaspoon garlic paste (or minced garlic)

¼ cup Italian parsley, chopped

1 teaspoon fennel seed

1 tablespoon olive oil

1 ½ cups heavy cream

1 cup mozzarella, shredded

¾ cup ricotta

1 egg, beaten

6 ounces lasagna sheets

Nonstick cooking spray

1. Preheat the oven to 350F. Place ground chicken, salt, ½ teaspoon pepper, garlic, Italian parsley, and fennel in a bowl and combine.

2. Heat olive oil in a skillet over medium heat and thoroughly cook the chicken. Set aside.

3. In a small pot, warm heavy cream over medium low. Add 1 cup Parmesan and remaining pepper until cheese melts. Set aside.

4. In a small bowl, combine the mozzarella, remaining Parmesan, ricotta, and egg.

5. Bring a large pot of salted water to a boil and cook lasagna sheets for 8 minutes. Drain lasagna sheets and cool.

6. Coat the inside of a loaf pan with cooking spray and add half of the cream sauce to the bottom of the pan.

7. Add one layer of lasagna sheets, cutting them to fit, if needed.

8. Spread ½ of the ricotta mixture evenly over the lasagna sheets, followed by ½ of the chicken.

9. Repeat the process, layering lasagna sheet, ricotta mixture, and chicken once more (2 layers in total).

10. Top with the remaining lasagna sheet, followed by the remaining cream sauce.

11. Bake, uncovered, until bubbling, about 30 minutes.

12. Allow the lasagna to set for 15 minutes before serving.

Bagna Cauda Mac and Cheese

American comfort food meets Piemonte's signature sauce! A staple in my family for generations, our family shared Bagna Cauda every New Year's Day to celebrate the year to come. Thickened with cream cheese, half-and-half, and parmesan, this is the mac-and-cheese reboot you've been dreaming about.

SERVES: 2 | PREP TIME: 5 MIN | COOK TIME: 15 MIN | TOTAL TIME: 20 MIN

8 ounces ditalini pasta

3 tablespoons butter

1 teaspoon garlic paste (or minced garlic)

2 tablespoons anchovy paste

1 cup half-and-half

2 teaspoons black pepper

½ cup sour cream

2 tablespoons cream cheese

¼ cup parmesan cheese

½ cup Italian shredded cheese blend (provolone, fontina, asiago, etc.)

2 tablespoons chives, diced

1. Boil 8 ounces of ditalini pasta for 10 minutes.

2. Melt butter over low heat. Add garlic and anchovy paste and gently stir until the anchovy paste disintegrates. Add half-and-half and increase heat to medium, whisking regularly for 4–5 minutes. Add black pepper, sour cream, cream cheese, parmesan cheese, and ½ cup of any variety of Italian shredded cheese blend. It may be a little thinner than you think a cheese sauce should be.

3. Drain your cooked ditalini and add your bagna cauda sauce. Top with diced chives.

Secondi

Welcome to the main event! Secondi, or "second plates," are entrées made with meat or seafood. Substantial plates that are well balanced and packed with flavor, each of these dishes boldly stands on its own.

Shevetone Meatballs

There's only one original meatball recipe in our house. This one.
No veal. No pork. All flavor. The breadcrumbs you choose make all the
difference. Buy the absolute best you can. They should be finely ground
(ultra-small crumbs) and very dry. Only then will you achieve a perfectly
roasted exterior that is unmistakably savory.

SERVES: 2 I PREP TIME: 5 MIN I COOK TIME: 25 MIN I TOTAL TIME: 30 MIN

1 pound ground beef

**1 cup seasoned Italian
breadcrumbs**

½ cup parmesan

1 egg

1 tablespoon soy sauce

1 teaspoon pepper

**3 tablespoons chopped Italian
parsley**

1. Preheat oven to 350F. Line a baking sheet with
    parchment or non-stick foil.

2. Roll beef mixture into 12 meatballs.

3. Bake for 25 minutes.

Manhattan BBQ Ribs

Classic Italian fare? No. But I've never met an Italian who doesn't genuinely adore fall-off-the-bone pork ribs. And when the barbecue sauce is made with a properly mixed Manhattan and caramelized into the meat? I'll say less.

SERVES: 2 | PREP TIME: 30 MIN | COOK TIME: 2.5 HRS | TOTAL TIME: 3 HRS

For the Manhattan BBQ Sauce:

1 cup ketchup

½ cup crushed tomatoes (or tomato passata/purée)

½ cup beef stock

¼ cup Worcestershire sauce

2 tablespoons brown coconut sugar (or light brown sugar)

2 tablespoons apple cider vinegar

1 teaspoon black pepper

1 tablespoon chili powder

¼ cup grated onion

1 tablespoon garlic paste (or minced garlic)

1 Manhattan Cocktail

For the Ribs:

1 rack baby back ribs

3 tablespoons favorite spice rub, such as steak or pork seasoning blend

To Make the Manhattan BBQ Sauce:

1. Combine all Manhattan BBQ sauce ingredients in a pot.

2. Simmer uncovered, stirring occasionally, until warmed and slightly thickened, 20–30 minutes.

To Make the Ribs:

1. Preheat oven to 300F.

2. Season baby back ribs, front and back, with about 3 tablespoons of your favorite spice rub.

3. Seal the rack completely in aluminum foil. Place on a baking sheet and bake for 2 hours.

4. Remove the ribs from the oven and fire up the BBQ. Take the foil off and let the ribs rest for 10 minutes or so.

5. Cut down cleanly between the bones and brush each rib with your luscious Manhattan BBQ sauce.

6. Grill the ribs until you see some nice charring, about 5 minutes per side.

Manhattan Cocktail

Make the Manhattan BBQ Ribs with my Manhattan Cocktail recipe on page 59.

Parmesan Chicken Patties

Didn't use all your ground chicken when you made Lasagne Bianche di Pollo? These patties are a cinch to make with parmesan and whole cream. Top with melted mozzarella and a dab of pesto (page 61).

SERVES: 2 | PREP TIME: 5 MIN | COOK TIME: 14 MIN | TOTAL TIME: 19 MIN

1 pound ground chicken breast

½ teaspoon salt

½ teaspoon pepper

⅓ cup pork rind crumbs

¼ cup heavy cream

1 egg

½ cup + 1 tablespoon grated parmesan

1 teaspoon garlic paste (or minced garlic)

¼ cup Italian parsley, chopped

½ teaspoon fennel seed

1 cup shredded mozzarella

2 tablespoons pesto

1. Preheat oven to 500F.

2. Place chicken in large mixing bowl. Add salt, pepper, pork rind crumbs, cream, egg, parmesan, garlic, parsley, and fennel.

3. Mix until combined and form 3 large thin patties.

4. Place patties on a parchment lined baking sheet and roast 12–15 minutes.

5. Top the roasted patties with mozzarella and place the patties back in oven to melt the cheese.

6. Garnish the patties with a dollop of pesto and the remaining parmesan.

Chicken Marinella

Staring at that raw chicken breast again, wondering what to make?
Marinara... mozzarella... Marinella!!

SERVES: 2 | PREP TIME: 10 MIN | COOK TIME: 45 MIN | TOTAL TIME: 55 MIN

2 boneless skinless chicken breasts

1 teaspoon salt

1 teaspoon Italian seasoning

½ teaspoon garlic powder

½ cup marinara sauce

½ cup shredded mozzarella

1. Preheat oven to 350F. Season the chicken on both sides with salt, Italian seasoning, and garlic powder. Place seasoned chicken on parchment-lined baking sheet; then spoon about 3–4 tablespoons of jarred marinara sauce on each breast (enough to cover each).

2. Bake for about 20–25 minutes (for thinner cutlets) to 35–40 minutes for larger breasts.

3. Once cooked, top with a layer of mozzarella (shredded or thin slices). Turn on your broiler and move your oven rack to the top.

4. Broil the cooked chicken to melt the cheese and slightly brown it, 1–2 minutes.

Easy Tomato Sauce

Make the Chicken Marinella with my delicious Easy Tomato Sauce recipe on page 63.

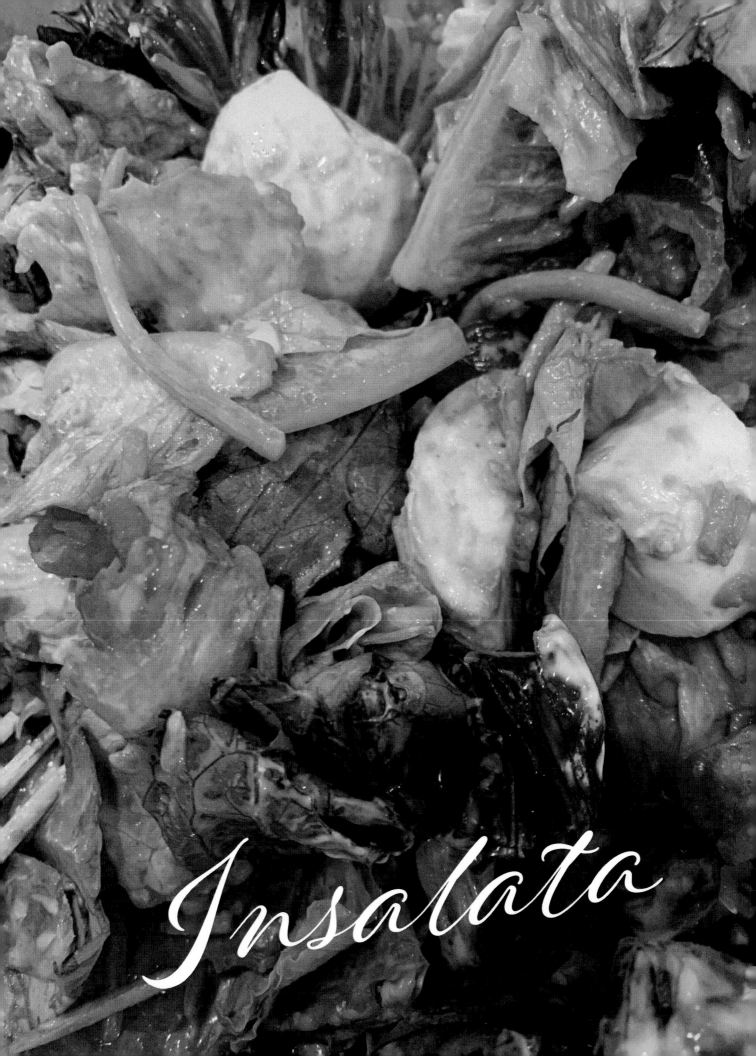

Insalata

Barring any leafy side dishes, or contorni, that are served with secondi, it's not uncommon for insalata—salad—to be served before dessert. Rich in fiber, authentic Italian salads are light, crisp, and believed to accelerate digestion. While the following insalata are far beyond mere palate cleansers, the ingredients can easily be scaled back to create lighter options when desired.

Buon Gusto Salad

When I first posted this salad on social media, I was overwhelmed by an avalanche of likes and hearts. In fact, the owner of a pizzeria chain on the East Coast messaged me that she was in search of the perfect salad, and planned to add it to her menu. (Do I get royalties?!)

SERVES: 2 | PREP TIME: 10 MIN | TOTAL TIME: 10 MIN

1 or 2 bags pre-washed lettuce (consider a combination of romaine and radicchio, 10-15 ounces)

1 cup sliced grape tomatoes

6 ounces salami, diced or sliced

½ cup artichoke hearts, quartered

½ Italian green olives

4 pepperoncini peppers, sliced

¼ cup shredded parmesan

1 teaspoon anchovy paste

3 tablespoons mayonnaise

2 tablespoons balsamic vinegar

Cracked black pepper

1. Place lettuce, tomatoes, salami, artichoke hearts, olives, peppers, and parmesan in a bowl and toss well.

2. Combine anchovy paste, mayonnaise, and balsamic vinegar, pour dressing over the salad and toss again. Season with cracked black pepper.

Piccata Pasta Salad

Didn't get enough pasta in Primi? This fresh pasta salad proves that piccata isn't just for protein. No mascarpone? A little cream cheese or mayonnaise will do in a pinch.

SERVES: 2 | PREP TIME: 5 MIN | COOK TIME: 10 MIN | TOTAL TIME: 15 MIN

8 ounces mini farfalle pasta

2 tablespoons mascarpone, room temperature

3 tablespoons butter, melted

2 tablespoons extra virgin olive oil

¼ cup lemon juice

3 tablespoons capers

3 tablespoons Italian parsley, chopped

½ teaspoon pepper

1. Boil pasta for 1–2 minutes longer than recommended cooking time, and drain.

2. While pasta is still warm, add mascarpone and mix well.

3. Combine butter, olive oil, lemon juice, and capers and add to the pasta. Garnish with parsley.

Spaghetti Western Caviar

This is what can happen when you accept a friend's dare to reinvent one of her favorite regional dishes. Challenge accepted: Cowboy caviar with an Italian flair!

SERVES: 2 | PREP TIME: 10 MIN | TOTAL TIME: 10 MIN

2 cups cooked black rice

1 can cannellini beans, drained and rinsed

1 cup cherry tomatoes, halved

2 tablespoons pimento

16 ½ ounce jar marinated artichoke hearts, drained and chopped

2 tablespoons champagne vinegar

2 tablespoons extra-virgin olive oil

1 teaspoon Italian seasoning

¼ teaspoon salt

½ teaspoon honey

1 teaspoon Dijon mustard

½ teaspoon ground black pepper

2 tablespoons celery leaves

2 tablespoons shredded parmesan

1. In a large bowl, stir together the black rice, cannellini beans, tomatoes, pimento, and artichoke hearts.

2. In a small bowl, whisk together the vinegar, olive oil, Italian seasoning, salt, honey, Dijon, and pepper. Pour the dressing over the bean mixture. Fold in the celery leaves and parmesan.

3. Refrigerate for an hour to allow the flavors to marry.

Insalata Rapida

No time? No problem! A few pulls from the fridge and you'll have a stunning salad that refreshes the palate. Bocconcini, delightful little balls of fresh mozzarella, can easily be swapped out for cubes of any cheese you have on hand.

SERVES: 2 | PREP TIME: 5 MIN | COOK TIME: 5 MIN | TOTAL TIME: 10 MIN

2 tablespoons balsamic vinegar

2 tablespoons mayonnaise

1 bag pre-washed Italian lettuce medley

¼ cup shredded carrots

4 ounces salami, diced

1 ounce prosciutto, diced

2 cup grape tomatoes, sliced

3 bocconcini, quartered or small mozzarella balls

1. Whisk balsamic vinegar and mayonnaise together in a small bowl.

2. Combine all ingredients and toss with dressing.

Dolce

Italian for "sweet," dolce is the course for which I gladly accept help from the grocery store. In the eyes of this lackadaisical baker, high-quality box mixes are readily available, immensely convenient, and nearly impossible to detect. While the increased number of servings presents a slight challenge, I'm generally excited to overcook when dessert is involved!

Strawberry Crostata

No matter what fruit is in season, take your pick of any frozen berries for this wonderfully rustic pie. Add a tablespoon of plum or blueberry preserves to accentuate the natural sweetness of any fruit. A few ribbons of mint, a sprinkle of zest, and satisfaction is sure to follow.

SERVES: 2 | PREP TIME: 5 MIN | COOK TIME: 25 MIN | TOTAL TIME: 30 MIN

1 store-bought, raw/thawed pie crust

10 ounces frozen strawberries, thawed and drained

1 tablespoon agave syrup

1 tablespoon coconut sugar

1 tablespoon lemon juice

½ teaspoon lemon zest

1. Preheat over to 400F and place a piece of parchment paper or aluminum foil on a sheet pan. Place raw pie crust on the parchment or foil.

2. Combine strawberries, agave syrup, coconut sugar, and lemon juice and place in the middle of your crust. Pull the crust in toward the filling, forming a border around the edge.

3. Bake for 20–30 minutes until crust is golden brown. Sprinkle lemon zest on crostata and serve warm.

Mina's Lemon Cake

My great-grandmother lovingly baked this cake for our family every week. Delightfully light and moist, Mina's Lemon Cake is the perfect treat when there are more than two at the table—or when you're alone and have been really, really good.

SERVES: 8 | PREP TIME: 5 MIN | COOK TIME: 40 MIN | TOTAL TIME: 45 MIN

1 box yellow cake mix

1 package lemon jello, powder only

4 eggs, beaten

¾ cup vegetable oil

¾ cup water

½ cup powdered sugar

½ cup lemon juice

1. Preheat oven to 325F. Combine cake mix, jello, eggs, oil, and water and beat together until well mixed.

2. Pour into greased 9x13 pan and bake for 35–40 minutes.

3. Remove cake from the oven and poke all over with a fork. Combine powdered sugar and lemon juice and drizzle over the cake while warm.

Polenta Dolce Due

Polenta dolce has been a fixture on our family's dessert table for well over 50 years. Made with Cream of Wheat® and flavored with lemon and almond extract, polenta dolce are fried, bite-sized, creamy pillows, dusted in sugar. In Italian, *due* means "two." This 2.0 version transforms the fried coating into a mouthwatering crust, is topped with deliciously creamy filling, and then finished with brûléed turbinado sugar.

SERVES: 2 | PREP TIME: 10 MIN | COOK TIME: 10 MIN | TOTAL TIME: 20 MIN
(plus 2 hrs chill time)

¾ cups Kellogg's® Corn Flakes® crumbs

3 tablespoons unsalted butter, melted

5 tablespoons granulated sugar

Nonstick cooking spray

2 ½ cups half-and-half

The zest of 1 lemon

½ cup 2½ Minute Cream of Wheat® (not instant)

¼ teaspoon of salt

1 ½ teaspoons almond extract

2 tablespoons lemon juice

4 tablespoons turbinado sugar (optional)

1. Mix the crumbs, melted butter, and 2 tablespoons of the granulated sugar together until combined. The mixture will be thick, coarse, and sandy.

2. Apply a light coating of nonstick cooking spray on the inside of two ramekins. Press half of the crumb mixture into the bottom of each ramekin and slightly up the sides. Chill the crust for 2 hours.

3. Warm the half-and-half over medium high heat and add the lemon zest. When it begins to boil, reduce heat to medium and slowly add cream of wheat, salt, and remaining sugar. Cook, whisking frequently, until mixture thickens, about 2 ½ minutes. Turn off the heat and whisk in the almond extract and lemon juice. Allow to cool for about 10 minutes.

4. Remove ramekins from the refrigerator and fill each to the top with the Cream of Wheat®.

5. **Optional:** To brûlée the top, sprinkle half the turbinado sugar on each ramekin and caramelize using a culinary/small torch. If you do not have a blowtorch, place the ramekins on a sheet pan and place under the broiler for 2–3 minutes.

Cannoli Brownies

Your favorite brownie mix will never be the same. Cannoli filling is transformed into a frosting so exquisite, you'll be asked to bring these brownies to every potluck, BBQ, and picnic until the world runs out of ricotta. If you're lucky enough to have cannoli shells, crack those over the top in lieu of fried wonton strips.

SERVES: 4 | PREP TIME: 10 MIN | COOK TIME: 30 MIN | TOTAL TIME: 40 MIN

1 box brownie mix

2 tablespoons maraschino cherry juice

15 ounces whole milk ricotta

1 tablespoon almond extract

½ cup mini milk chocolate chips

1 cup powdered sugar

Maraschino cherries (optional)

Fried wonton pieces (optional)

1. Prepare brownies as directed, but replace 2 tablespoons of water (from box recipe) with maraschino cherry juice (right from the jar in the fridge).

2. Bake as directed and allow to cool for at least 20 minutes.

3. For the frosting, mix ricotta with almond extract, mini milk chocolate chips, and powdered sugar. Frost cooked, cooled brownies with this delectable cannoli "filling," then chill in the fridge for about 30 minutes.

4. **Optional**—but adorable! Decorate with mini chocolate chips, maraschino cherries, and fried wonton pieces to mimic cannoli shells.

Supplementare

Who doesn't love another helping from time to time? This chapter offers additional recipes that will be helpful as you prepare many of the dishes in this cookbook.

Manhattan Cocktail

Whether you prefer them perfect or imperfect, Manhattans are the quintessential bourbon martini. Don't forget to make extra for your Manhattan BBQ Sauce (page 31)!

SERVES: 2 | PREP TIME: 5 MIN | TOTAL TIME: 5 MIN

4 ounces bourbon

1 ounce Sweet Vermouth

1 ounce Dry Vermouth

1. Combine all ingredients in a pitcher over ice.

2. Stir, strain, and divide into 2 martini glasses, garnishing each with a maraschino cherry.

Pesto

Derived from the Italian verb *pestare* ("to pound or crush"), traditional Genoese pesto can be adapted in infinite ways using a variety of nuts and greens to complement your dishes. Don't have pine nuts?
Try almonds!

SERVES: 2 | PREP TIME: 5 MIN | COOK TIME: 5 MIN | TOTAL TIME: 10 MIN

1 cup fresh basil

**1 teaspoon garlic paste
 (or minced garlic)**

½ cup parmesan cheese

⅓ cup pine nuts

¼-½ cup extra virgin olive oil

1. Add basil, garlic, parmesan, and pine nuts to a food processor.

2. Slowly drizzle the olive oil until it reaches your desired consistency.

Easy Tomato Sauce

This classic sauce pairs beautifully with Chicken Marinella (page 35). Making a pizza? Skip the 15-minute simmer step and add the tomato paste, garlic, tomatoes, and seasoning to a blender and pulse until smooth.

SERVES: 2-4 | PREP TIME: 5 MIN | COOK TIME: 15 MIN | TOTAL TIME: 20 MIN

1 tablespoon extra virgin olive oil

1 teaspoon garlic paste (or minced garlic)

1 teaspoon tomato paste

1 28-ounce can San Marzano tomatoes (or a 24-ounce bottle passata/tomato puree)

1 teaspoon salt

1 teaspoon Italian seasoning

Ground pepper, to taste

1. Heat up some extra virgin oil over medium heat. Once hot, put a teaspoon of garlic and a teaspoon of tomato paste and toast for about 30 seconds.

2. Drain tomatoes, and add to pot. Add salt, Italian seasoning, and several grinds of pepper.

3. Reduce to low heat and simmer for 15 minutes, stirring every 3–4 minutes.

Bagna Cauda

Piemonte's pride and joy, this buttery condiment has been relished by Northern Italians for centuries. Traditionally served warm with crudités and bread, the addition of sour cream is optional but serves as a lovely counterbalance for those who don't [think they] like anchovies.

SERVES: 2 | PREP TIME: 5 MIN | COOK TIME: 5 MIN | TOTAL TIME: 10 MIN

4 tablespoons butter

**1 teaspoon garlic paste
(or minced garlic)**

2 tablespoons anchovy paste

½ cup sour cream

1. Melt butter over low heat.

2. Add garlic and anchovy paste and gently stir until the anchovy paste disintegrates.

3. Add sour cream and stir until fully combined.

Published in the United States by Dink Cuisine LLC, Las Vegas.
dinkcuisine.com
Names: Shevetone, Alicia, author.
Title: Italian Recipes for Two / Alicia Shevetone
Subjects: LCSH Cooking, Cooking for two; Cooking, Italian; Cooking,
Italian—Northern style
Book and Cover Design: Stephanie Triplett
Editor: Traci Keller
Cover Photography: David Sadleir
First Edition

Made in the USA
Las Vegas, NV
24 June 2024

91448486R00040